# 100 BEST CHRISTMAS POEMS FOR CHILDREN

Roger McGough CBE, FRSL is one of our most popular poets, having published over fifty books of poetry for both adults and children. He came to prominence in the 1960s with the publication of *The Mersey Sound*, which has sold over a million copies and is now published as a Penguin Classic. The winner of two BAFTAs for his film work, and a Royal Television Society Award, McGough has also won a Cholmondeley Award from the Society of Authors and is twice winner of both the Signal and CLPE Awards for the best book of poetry for children. He presents *Poetry Please* on Radio 4 and is President of the Poetry Society. He was honoured with the Freedom of the City of Liverpool in 2001 and with a CBE in 2005 for services to literature.

# 100 BEST CHRISTMAS POEMS FOR CHILDREN

Edited by
## Roger McGough

ILLUSTRATED BY BEATRIZ CASTRO

First published in Great Britain in 2021

Society for Promoting Christian Knowledge
36 Causton Street
London SW1P 4ST
www.spck.org.uk

*British Library Cataloguing-in-Publication Data*
A catalogue record for this book is available from the British Library

ISBN 978–0–281–08469–2
eBook ISBN 978–0–281–08470–8

Designed and typeset by SPCK
First printed in Great Britain by Jellyfish Print Solutions

eBook by Manila Typesetting Company

Produced on paper from sustainable forests

# Contents

# Introduction

An anthology is the way in to poetry for many children. The variety of voices and tone, the modern and the classical in a single volume for the young reader to either stop, read and enjoy, or, puzzled, pass quickly on.

I have over the years compiled a number of anthologies, both for adults and for children, and have always cast my net as wide as possible to include poems and poets that were new to me. I cannot claim the full credit, however, for this compilation, and must acknowledge the help of my editor at SPCK, Philip Law. Our initial aim in 2019 was to invite schools all over the UK to submit their favourite Christmas poems, from which he and I would simply select 100. You know what happened next. The following year, something came along that nobody wanted for Christmas. So, Philip bravely stepped in to take up the reins, me following, masked, and safely distanced.

If poems were gifts, and in many ways they are, children will find plenty to absorb and amuse them in this bulging stocking of an anthology. Presents that will amuse from the likes of Ogden Nash, U. A. Fanthorpe and Paul Cookson, ones that make us see the familiar in a new and different way (Ted Hughes, Brian Patten, Coral Rumble), ones that take us back through time to a place of miracles (Christina Rossetti, William Blake, Laurie Lee).

If I go back through time to my first Christmas, it would be to the beginning of World War Two, and the place would be Liverpool. As you know, or can imagine, a sense of

encroaching disaster prevailed; there was fear and poverty.
And yet, we celebrated Christmas, a brief moment of joy,
a candle of faith in a darkness that seemed without end.
By acknowledging the Christmas narrative and celebrating
it we continue to help each other in similarly dark times.

Christmas is, of course, a religious festival for Christians all
over the world, but the message of hope, forgiveness and love
at its centre means that it is for everyone.

As are these poems.

*Roger McGough*

# One:
# The Season To Be Young

## 1. Winter Morning

Winter is the king of showmen,
Turning tree stumps into snowmen
And houses into birthday cakes
And spreading sugar over lakes.
Smooth and clean and frosty white,
The world looks good enough to bite.
That's the season to be young,
Catching snowflakes on your tongue.

Snow is snowy when it's snowing,
I'm sorry it's slushy when it's going.

*Ogden Nash*

## 2. Snow Clouds

Like sulky polar bears
Clouds prowl across the winter sky
From cold and snowy northern lands
As though from icy lairs.

Soon snow begins to fall –
Small snippets of the whitest fur
And like the stealthy polar bear
It makes no sound at all.

*Daphne Lister*

## 3. The Coming of the Cold

The ribs of leaves lie in the dust,
The beak of frost has pecked the bough,
The briar bears its thorn, and drought
Has left its ravage on the field.
The season's wreckage lies about,
Late autumn fruit is rotted now.
All shade is lean, the antic branch
Jerks skyward at the touch of wind,
Dense trees no longer hold the light,
The hedge and orchard grove are thinned.
The dank bark dries beneath the sun,
The last of harvesting is done.

All things are brought to barn and fold.
The oak leaves strain to be unbound,
The sky turns dark, the year grows old,
The buds draw in before the cold.

The small brook dies within its bed;
The stem that holds the bee is prone;
Old hedgerows keep the leaves; the phlox,
That late autumnal bloom, is dead.

All summer green is now undone:
The hills are grey, the trees are bare,
The mould upon the branch is dry,
The fields are harsh and bare, the rocks
Gleam sharply on the narrow sight.

The land is desolate, the sun
No longer gilds the scene at noon;
Winds gather in the north and blow
Bleak clouds across the heavy sky,
And frost is marrow-cold, and soon
Winds bring a fine and bitter snow.

*Theodore Roethke*

## 4. Somewhere around Christmas

Always, or nearly always, on old apple trees,
Somewhere around Christmas, if you look up through the frost,
You will see, fat as a bullfinch, stuck on a high branch,
One lingering, bald, self-sufficient, hard, blunt fruit.

There will be no leaves, you can be sure of that;
The twigs will be tar-black, and the white sky
Will be grabbed among the branches like thumbed glass
In broken triangles just saved from crashing to the ground.

11

Further up, dribbles of rain will run down
Like spilt colourless varnish on a canvas. The old tins,
Tyres, cardboard boxes, debris of back gardens,
Will lie around, bleak, with mould and rust creeping over them.

Blow on your fingers. Wipe your feet on the mat by the back door.
You will never see that apple fall. Look at the cat,
Her whiskers twitch as she sleeps by the kitchen fire;
In her backyard prowling dream she thinks it's a bird.

*John Smith*


## 5. Christmas at Four Winds Farm

With the tambourine tinkle of ice on the moor
and the winter moon white as a bone,
my grandad and his father
set out to bring Christmas home.

A wild winter wizard had grizzled the gorse
and spangled the splinter-sharp leaves,
when the light of their wind-swinging lantern
found a magical Christmas tree.

From the glittering town at the end of the dale
the carols grew sweeter and bolder,
as my grandad's smiling father
carried Christmas home on his shoulder.

*Maureen Haselhurst*

## 6. The Christmas Life

Bring in a tree, a young Norwegian spruce,
Bring hyacinths that rooted in the cold,
Bring winter jasmine as its buds unfold:
Bring the Christmas life into this house.

Bring red and green and gold, bring things that shine,
Bring candlesticks and music, food and wine.
Bring in your memories of Christmas past,
Bring in your tears for all that you have lost.

Bring in the shepherd boy, the ox and ass,
Bring in the stillness of an icy night,
Bring in a birth, of hope and love and light:
Bring the Christmas life into this house.

*Wendy Cope*

## 7. Street Lights

The town leapt a little, tonight,
As the Christmas lights came on.
Everyday streets became more important
And even the darkest pathways glistened.
Stars and snowflakes
Angels and reindeer
Flashed and flickered a holy-white whisper,
Making our town,
Our ordinary, brick and tarmac town,
Sparkle like a frosted castle
In a far-off, frozen land.

*Coral Rumble*

## 8. The Carol Singers

Last night the carol-singers came
    When I had gone to bed,
Upon the crisp white path outside
    I heard them softly tread.

I sat upright to listen, for
    I knew they came to tell,
Of all the things that happened on
    The very first Noel.

Upon my ceiling flickering
    I saw their lantern glow,
And then they sang their carols sweet
    Of Christmas long ago.

And when at last they went away,
    Their carol-singing done,
There was a little boy who wished
    They'd only just begun.

*Margaret G. Rhodes*

## 9. Sir Winter

I heard Sir Winter coming,
He crept out of his bed
and rubbed his thin and freezing hands:
'I'll soon be up!' he said.

'I'll shudder at the keyhole
and rattle at the door,
I'll strip the trees of all their leaves
and strew them on the floor.

'I'll harden every puddle
that Autumn thinks is his –
I'll lay a sparkling quilt of snow
on everything that is!

'I'll bring a load of darkness
as large as any coal,
and drive my husky dogs across
the world, from pole to pole.

'Oho! How you will shiver!'
– And then I heard him say;
'But in the middle of it all
I'll give you
        CHRISTMAS DAY!'

*Jean Kenward*

## 10. The Christmas Shed

It was late afternoon on Christmas Day
with light fading and flakes falling
when the three of us raced through the copse
where rhododendrons and holly bushes
bent low under their burden of fresh snow.
Gasping, we skidded to a stop
at the edge of the estate's allotments.
A bitter, whining wind made us shiver
as it whipped across the frozen earth.
  *'No one's about.*
  *Come on!'*

Slipping and skating we dashed for Jacko's shed
and at the back crawled through a hole
where the old boards had rotted away.
Inside it was dry. The air was still.
We peered as daylight filtered dimly
through the fly-spattered, cobwebbed window,
and breathed the shed's special smell
of pine, creosote, paraffin, and sawdust.
Fear of discovery made us whisper.
  *'Let's see if they're*
  *still there.'*

Carefully we moved garden implements
that were stacked in a corner.
Dried soil fell and crunched beneath our boots
as we shifted rakes, forks, spades, and hoes,
and *there* was Smoky and her four kittens
warm in a bed of worn gloves and jerseys.
Like the Three Kings we knelt and offered
our Christmas gifts – turkey scraps, ham, a sausage.
Smoky arched and purred and ate hungrily.
　　*'The kittens*
　　*are still blind.'*

The food vanished. We watched in silence
as the grey cat lay down and her mewling kittens
guzzled greedily at the milk bar.
　　*'It's late.'*
We replaced the implements
and crept out of Jacko's old shed.
Like shadows we hared for the cover of the copse.
Chilled to the bone we reached our estate
where Christmas lights were flashing. We split.
　　*'Same time tomorrow?'*
　　*'Yeah.'*
　　*'See you.'*

*Wes Magee*

# Two:
# Snowing, Snowing, Snowing

### 11. At Nine of the Night I Opened My Door

At nine of the night I opened my door
That stands midway between moor and moor,
And all around me, silver-bright,
I saw that the world had turned to white.

Thick was the snow on field and hedge
And vanished was the river-sedge,
Where winter skilfully had wound
A shining scarf without a sound.

And as I stood and gazed my fill
A stable boy came down the hill.
With every step I saw him take
Flew at his heel a puff of flake.

His brow was whiter than the hoar,
A beard of freshest snow he wore,
And round about him, snowflake starred,
A red horse-blanket from the yard.

In a red cloak I saw him go,
His back was bent, his step was slow,
And as he laboured through the cold
He seemed a hundred winters old.

I stood and watched the snowy head,
The whiskers white, the cloak of red.
'A Merry Christmas!' I heard him cry.
'The same to you, old friend,' said I.

*Charles Causley*

## 12. Snow and Snow

Snow is sometimes a she, a soft one.
    Her kiss on your cheek, her finger on your sleeve
In early December, on a warm evening.
    And you turn to meet her, saying 'It's snowing!'
        But it is not. And nobody's there.
        Empty and calm is the air.

Sometimes the snow is a he, a sly one.
    Weakly he signs the dry stone with a damp spot.
Waifish he floats and touches the pond and is not.
    Treacherous-beggarly he falters, and taps at the window.
        A little longer he clings to the grass-blade tip
        Getting his grip.

Then how she leans, how furry foxwrap she nestles
    The sky with her warm, and the earth with her softness.
How her lit crowding fairytales sink through the space-silence
    To build her palace, till it twinkles in starlight –
        Too frail for a foot
        Or a crumb of soot.

Then how his muffled armies move in all night
    And we wake and every road is blockaded
Every hill taken and every farm occupied
    And the white glare of his tents is on the ceiling.
      And all that dull blue day and on into the gloaming
      We have to watch more coming.

Then everything in the rubbish-heaped world
    Is a bridesmaid at her miracle.
Dunghills and crumbly dark old barns are bowed in the chapel of
her sparkle,
    The gruesome boggy cellars of the wood
      Are a wedding of lace
      Now taking place.

*Ted Hughes*

## 13. First Snow in the Street

I did not sleep last night.
The falling snow was beautiful and white.
I dressed, sneaked down the stairs
And opened wide the door.
I had not seen such snow before.

Our grubby little street had gone.
The world was brand-new, and everywhere
There was pureness in the air.
I felt such peace. Watching every flake
My heart felt more and more awake.

I thought I'd learned all there was to know
About the trillion million different kinds
Of swirling frosty falling flakes of snow.
But that was not so.
I did not know how vividly it lit
The world with such a peaceful glow.

Upstairs my parents slept,
Yet I could not drag myself away from that sight
To call them down and have them share
The mute miracle that was everywhere.
The snow seemed to fall for me alone.
How beautiful the grubby little street had grown!

*Brian Patten*

## 14. Winter Morning

No one has ever been here before,
Never before!
Snow is stretching, pure and white,
From the back door
To where that elm-tree by the coppice-fence
Stands black and bare,
With never a footprint, never a clawprint
Anywhere!
Only the clean, white page of snow
In front of me,
With the long shadow of a single tree
For company.

*Clive Sansom*


## 15. When All the World Is Full of Snow

I never know
just where to go,
when all the world
is full of snow.

I do not want
to make a track,
not even
to the shed and back.

I only want
to watch and wait,
while snow moths settle
on the gate,

and swarming frost flakes
fill the trees
with billions
of albino bees.

I want to watch
the snow swarms thin,
'til all my bees
have settled in,

and on the ice
the boulders ride,
like sleeping snow geese
on the tide.

I only want
myself to be
as silent as
a winter tree,

to hear the swirling
stillness grow,
when all the world
is full of snow.

*N. M. Bodecker*

## 16. The North Wind

The North Wind does blow
And we shall have snow,
And what will the robin do then,
    Poor thing?
He'll sit in a barn
And keep himself warm,
And hide his head under his wing.
    Poor thing.

*Anonymous*

## 17. Robin's Song

Robins sang in England,
    Frost or rain or snow,
All the long December days
    Endless years ago.

Robins sang in England
    Before the Legions came,
Before our English fields were tilled
    Or England was a name.

Robins sang in England
    When forests dark and wild
Stretched across from sea to sea
    And Jesus was a child.

Listen! In the frosty dawn
    From his leafless bough
The same brave song he ever sang
    A robin's singing now.

*Rodney Bennett*

## 18. Snowing

Snowing. Snowing. Snowing.
Woolly petals tossed down
From a tremendous tree in the sky
By a giant hand, the hand
That switches on lightning
And tips down cloudbursts.
I like to think of it that way.

Quiet. Quiet. Quiet.
No noise of traffic in the street.
In the classroom only Miss Nil's voice
Dictating and the rustle of paper.
I am holding my breath in wonder.
I want to cry out 'Look! Look!'
Miss Nil has paused between sentences
And is looking out of the window.
But I suppose she is wondering whether
She'll have to abandon her car and walk home.

Snowing. Snowing. Snowing.
I wish I could go out and taste it.
Feel it nestling against my cheek.
And trickling through my fingers.
The message has come round we are to go home now
Because the buses may stop running.
So the snow has given us a whole hour of freedom.
I pick up fistfuls.
Squeeze them hard and hurl them.

But hurry, the bus is coming
And I want to get home early to look at the garden:
At the holly tree in its polar bear coat;
The cherries with white arms upstretched,
Naked of leaves; the scratchy claw marks
Of birds, and blobs of big pawed dogs.
And I want to make footprints of my own
Where the snow is a blank page for scribbling.
Tea time already. Still the snow comes down.
Migrating moths, millions and millions
Dizzying down out of the darkening sky.

Mother draws the curtains.
Why couldn't they stay open?
Now I can't watch the secretive birds
Descending, the stealthy army invading.
What does the roof look like
Covered with slabs of cream?
How high are the heaps on window ledges?
Tomorrow the snow may have begun to melt away.
Why didn't I look more
While there was still time?

*Olive Dove*

## 19. The Land of Snow

Snow ... snow ... eternally falling:
Armies in white, crossing the grey-blue air
In endless downward procession, falling and falling.

Snow on the swift deer, the running deer of the forest;
On sledges that travel the hidden roads faster than wolves that
follow;
Snow on a frozen lake and the Snow Queen's palace of ice.

All is a world of whiteness: Earth with her winter blossom,
Sky her incessant snowflakes ... Ah, but look
Forging south, opposing the white relentless legions,
There flies a single crow, calling and calling.

*Clive Sansom*

## 20. The Snowman

Child's play:
stacked snow,
scarf, hat,
carrot nose,
stick and
round pebbles
for eyes.

He freezes:
fat target
for snowballers
who dearly
want to
knock off
his block.

Three days,
and grey
with age
he shrinks
as warmth
turns the
world green.

Scarf, hat
are reclaimed.
Pebbles mark
his grave,
damp lawn
where a
child plays.

*Wes Magee*

## 21. Snow Joke

Why does it have to be Snowmen?
Why is it never Snowgirls?
Why can't we build a Snow-princess
With berries for rubies and pearls?
Why can't we pick her some holly
And give her a spiky, green crown?
What about icicle diamonds
To wear on her glittering gown?
What about crowds of Snow-ladies
With twiggy and twizzly curls?
Why does it have to be Snowmen?
Why is it NEVER Snowgirls?

*Clare Bevan*

## 22. Christmas Cat

I've built a cuddly snowcat
With whiskers made from straws –
And I'm almost sure,
I'm *almost* sure
I saw him lick his paws.

He's sitting in my garden,
He's smiling at me now,
And I'm almost sure,
I'm *almost* sure
I heard him say, 'Mee-ow!'

*Clare Bevan*

## 23. Haiku

Snowman in a field
listening to the raindrops
wishing him farewell

*Roger McGough*

# Three:
# When God Lay In His
# Mother's Arms

### 24. Mary's Burden

My Baby, my Burden,
    To-morrow the morn
I shall go lighter
    And you will be born.

I shall go lighter,
    But heavier too
For seeing the burden,
    That falls upon you.

The burden of love,
    The burden of pain,
I'll see you bear both
    Among men once again.

To-morrow you'll bear it
    Your burden alone,
To-night you've no burden
    That is not my own.

My Baby, my Burden,
    To-morrow the morn
I shall go lighter
    And you will be born.

*Eleanor Farjeon*


## 25. The Innkeeper of Bethlehem

'There's no room at the inn,' he told them.
'We're full up, I am sorry to say.
Inn's crammed with people. Can't help it.
I'm having to turn folk away.'
But there was something about the young woman
and the innkeeper shouted out, 'Wait.
I suppose you could sleep in the stable,
there's nothing else left, and it's late.'
He showed them both round to the stable
and settled them down for the night,
then he left, glancing up at the heavens
where a star shone unnaturally bright,
gilding his face with a splendour
that no one on earth ever saw
as he entered his inn, slightly dazzled,
quietly closing the door.

*Marian Swinger*

## 26. Something Beautiful and New and Strange
## (from *The Witnesses*)

*The Innkeeper's wife*:
It was a night in winter.
Our house was full, tight-packed as salted herrings –
So full, they said, we had to hold our breaths
To close the door and shut the night-air out!
And then two travellers came. They stood outside
Across the threshold, half in the ring of light
And half beyond it. I would have let them in
Despite the crowding – the woman was past her time –
But I'd no mind to argue with my husband,
The flagon in my hand and half the inn
Still clamouring for wine. But when trade slackened,
And all our guests had sung themselves to bed
Or told the floor their troubles, I came out here
Where he had lodged them. The man was standing
As you are now, his hand smoothing that board.
He was a carpenter, I heard them say.
She rested on the straw, and on her arm
A child was lying. None of your creased-faced brats
Squalling their lungs out. Just lying there
As calm as a new-dropped calf – his eyes wide open,
And gazing round as if the world he saw
In the chaff-strewn light of the stable lantern
Was something beautiful and new and strange.

*Clive Sansom*

## 27. Listen

Listen.
Far away, the snort of a camel,
The swish of boots in the endless sand,
The whisper of silk and the clatter of ceremonial swords,
Far away.

Listen.
Not so far, the slam of a castle door,
A cry of rage on the midnight air,
A jangle of spurs and the cold thrust of a soldier's command,
Not so far.

Listen.
Closer now, the homely bleat of a ewe among the grasses,
The answering call of her lamb, fresh born,
The rattle of stones on a hillside path,
Closer now.

Listen.
Closer still, the murmur of women in the dark,
The kindly creak of a stable door,
The steady breathing of the sleepy beasts,
Closer still.

Listen.
So close you are almost there,
The singing of the stars,
The soundless flurry of wings,
The soft whimper of a child amongst the straw,
So close you are almost there.

*Clare Bevan*

## 28. Cradle Hymn

Away in a manger, no crib for a bed,
The little Lord Jesus laid down his sweet head.
The stars in the bright sky looked down where he lay,
The little Lord Jesus asleep on the hay.

The cattle are lowing, the baby awakes,
But little Lord Jesus no crying he makes.
I love thee, Lord Jesus! look down from the sky,
And stay by my cradle till morning is nigh.

Be near me, Lord Jesus, I ask thee to stay
Close by me for ever and love me, I pray.
Bless all the dear children in thy tender care,
And fit us for heaven, to live with thee there.

*Traditional*

## 29. Joseph

I am Joseph, carpenter,
Of David's kingly line,
I wanted an heir; discovered
My wife's son wasn't mine.

I am an obstinate lover,
Loved Mary for better or worse.
Wouldn't stop loving when I found
Someone Else came first.

Mine was the likeness I hoped for
When the first-born man-child came.
But nothing of him was me. I couldn't
Even choose his name.

I am Joseph, who wanted
To teach my own boy how to live.
My lesson for my foster son:
Endure. Love. Give.

*U. A. Fanthorpe*

This was the moment when Before
Turned into After, and the future's
Uninvented timekeepers presented arms.

This was the moment when nothing
Happened. Only dull peace
Sprawled boringly over the earth.

This was the moment when even energetic Romans
Could find nothing better to do
Than counting heads in remote provinces.

And this was the moment
When a few farm workers and three
Members of an obscure Persian sect

Walked haphazard by starlight straight
Into the kingdom of heaven.

*U. A. Fanthorpe*

## 31. Shepherd's Song at Christmas

Look there at the star!
I, among the least,
Will arise and take
A journey to the East.
*But what shall I bring*
*As a present for the King?*
*What shall I bring to the Manger?*

    I will bring a song,
    A song that I will sing,
    A song for the King
    In the Manger.

Watch out for my flocks,
Do not let them stray.
I am going on a journey
Far, far away.
*But what shall I bring*
*As a present for the Child?*
*What shall I bring to the Manger?*

    I will bring a lamb,
    Gentle, meek, and mild,
    A lamb for the Child
    In the Manger.

I'm just a shepherd boy,
Very poor I am –
But I know there is
A King in Bethlehem.
*What shall I bring*
*As a present just for Him?*
*What shall I bring to the Manger?*

I will bring my heart
And give my heart to Him.
I will bring my heart
To the Manger.

*Langston Hughes*

## 32. The Shepherds' Carol

We stood on the hills, Lady,
Our day's work done,
Watching the frosted meadows
That winter had won.

The evening was calm, Lady,
The air so still.
Silence more lovely than music
Folded the hill.

There was a star, Lady,
Shone in the night,
Larger than Venus it was
And bright, so bright.

Oh, a voice from the sky, Lady,
It seemed to us then
Telling of God being born
In the world of men.

And so we have come, Lady,
Our day's work done.
Our love, our hopes, ourselves
We give to your son.

*Traditional*

## 33. The Three Kings

Three Kings came riding from far away,
    Melchior and Gaspar and Baltasar;
Three Wise Men out of the East were they,
And they travelled by night and they slept by day,
    For their guide was a beautiful, wonderful star.

The star was so beautiful, large, and clear,
    That all the other stars of the sky
Became a white mist in the atmosphere,
And by this they knew that the coming was near
    Of the Prince foretold in the prophecy.

Three caskets they bore on their saddle-bows,
    Three caskets of gold with golden keys;
Their robes were of crimson silk with rows
Of bells and pomegranates and furbelows,
    Their turbans like blossoming almond-trees.

And so the Three Kings rode into the West,
    Through the dusk of night, over hill and dell,
And sometimes they nodded with beard on breast,
And sometimes talked, as they paused to rest,
    With the people they met at some wayside well.

'Of the child that is born,' said Baltasar,
    'Good people, I pray you, tell us the news;
For we in the East have seen his star,
And have ridden fast, and have ridden far,
    To find and worship the King of the Jews.'

And the people answered, 'You ask in vain;
    We know of no king but Herod the Great!'
They thought the Wise Men were men insane,
As they spurred their horses across the plain,
    Like riders in haste, and who cannot wait.

And when they came to Jerusalem,
    Herod the Great, who had heard this thing,
Sent for the Wise Men and questioned them;
And said, 'Go down unto Bethlehem,
    And bring me tidings of this new king.'

So they rode away; and the star stood still,
    The only one in the gray of morn;
Yes, it stopped, – it stood still of its own free will,
Right over Bethlehem on the hill,
    The city of David, where Christ was born.

And the Three Kings rode through the gate and the guard,
    Through the silent street, till their horses turned
And neighed as they entered the great inn-yard;
But the windows were closed, and the doors were barred,
    And only a light in the stable burned.

And cradled there in the scented hay,
    In the air made sweet by the breath of kine,
The little child in the manger lay,
The child, that would be king one day
    Of a kingdom not human but divine.

His mother Mary of Nazareth
    Sat watching beside his place of rest,
Watching the even flow of his breath,
For the joy of life and the terror of death
    Were mingled together in her breast.

They laid their offerings at his feet:
    The gold was their tribute to a King,
The frankincense, with its odor sweet,
Was for the Priest, the Paraclete,
    The myrrh for the body's burying.

And the mother wondered and bowed her head,
    And sat as still as a statue of stone;
Her heart was troubled yet comforted,
Remembering what the Angel had said
    Of an endless reign and of David's throne.

Then the Kings rode out of the city gate,
    With a clatter of hoofs in proud array;
But they went not back to Herod the Great
For they knew his malice and feared his hate,
    And returned to their homes by another way.

*Henry Wadsworth Longfellow*

## 34. Balthasar: 'A Cold Coming We Had of It'
## ('Journey of the Magi', T S Eliot)

Yes. It was cold. Of course. Specially the nights.
But we had furs and tents, good fires and lights.
The camel-men were unruly – but they always are;
You couldn't really complain. And that fantastic star
Impressed even them. Melchior kept on about the cold
But he wasn't well, and face it, he was too old
For such a journey. For Caspar and me though, I'd say
It was a true adventure! So exciting! A great day
For astrology too! Just as we'd predicted. Everything!
Time. Place, Birth, Animals. It's true. The King
Wasn't quite what we'd thought, a bit of a disappointment.
But we left our gifts, the gold, the herbs, the ointment,
Made our speeches. The mother didn't seem too amazed,
Seemed to have expected us. – And no. It hasn't raised
The profile of astrology. A good thirty years have passed
And what with these Jerusalem riots, all that has got lost.
But I shan't forget the absolute delight
Of that strange journey. And we were all three quite
Certain something world-changing had happened that night.

*Gerard Benson*

## 35. The Adoration of the Magi

It was the arrival of the kings
that caught us unawares;
we'd looked in on the woman in the barn,
curiosity you could call it,
something to do on a cold winter's night;
we'd wished her well –
that was the best we could do, she was in pain,
and the next thing we knew
she was lying on the straw
– the little there was of it –
and there was this baby in her arms.

It was, as I say, the kings
that caught us unawares ...
Women have babies every other day,
not that we are there –
let's call it a common occurrence though,
giving birth. But kings
appearing in a stable with a
'Is this the place?' and kneeling,
each with his gift held out towards the child!

50

They didn't even notice us.
Their robes trailed on the floor,
rich, lined robes that money couldn't buy.
What must this child be
to bring kings from distant lands
with costly incense and gold?
What could a tiny baby make of that?

And what were we to make of
was it angels falling through the air,
entwined and falling as if from the rafters
to where the gaze of the kings met the child's
– assuming the child could see?

What would the mother do with the gift?
What would become of the child?
And we'll never admit there are angels

or that somewhere between
one man's eyes and another's
is a holy place, a space where a king could be
at one with a naked child,
at one with an astonished soldier.

*Christopher Pilling*

## 36. I Never Trusted Herod

With his bright beady eye
With his slippery pink smile
And his, 'See you bye and bye ...'
I never trusted Herod,
So why, oh why,
Did I tell him what I knew
Of the star in the sky?
I never trusted Herod
With his hand on my arm
Promising he meant the best
Saying 'There's no harm ...'
I never trusted Herod
But I blabbed just the same
Shot my mouth off, said too much
And so I feel to blame
For what happened – for the soldiers,
When finally they came ...

I dream a lot of Herod
I dream we never met,
And all those little children
Are happy – living yet.
In my dreams the snow shines white.
The ice does not melt red
But when I wake I find
That still the dead are dead.

And the baby? Did he find him?
We left so fast – I never knew.
The baby underneath the star,
Did they kill him too?

*Jan Dean*

## 37. In the Bleak Midwinter

In the bleak midwinter
Frosty wind made moan,
Earth stood hard as iron,
Water like a stone;
Snow had fallen, snow on snow,
Snow on snow,
In the bleak midwinter
Long ago.

Our God, Heaven cannot hold Him,
Nor earth sustain;
Heaven and earth shall flee away
When He comes to reign.
In the bleak midwinter
A stable place sufficed
The Lord God Almighty,
Jesus Christ.

Enough for Him, whom cherubim
Worship night and day,
A breastful of milk,
And a mangerful of hay;
Enough for Him, whom angels
Fall down before,
The ox and ass and camel
Which adore.

Angels and archangels
May have gathered there,
Cherubim and seraphim
Thronged the air;
But His mother only,
In her maiden bliss,
Worshipped the beloved
With a kiss.

What can I give Him,
Poor as I am?
If I were a shepherd,
I would bring a lamb;
If I were a Wise Man,
I would do my part;
Yet what I can I give Him:
Give my heart.

*Christina Rossetti*

## 38. Nativity in 20 Seconds

Silent night
Candle light
Holy bright

Stable poor
Prickly straw
Donkey snore

Babe asleep
Lambs leap
Shepherds peep

Star guide
Kings ride
Manger side

Angels wing
Bells ring
Children sing
WELCOME KING!

*Coral Rumble*

## 39. Christmas Morning

If Bethlehem were here today,
Or this were very long ago,
There wouldn't be a winter time
Nor any cold or snow.

I'd run out through the garden gate,
And down along the pasture walk;
And off beside the cattle barns
I'd hear a kind of gentle talk.

I'd move the heavy iron chain
And pull away the wooden pin;
I'd push the door a little bit
And tiptoe very softly in.

The pigeons and the yellow hens
And all the cows would stand away;
Their eyes would open wide to see
A lady in the manger hay,

If this were very long ago
And Bethlehem were here today.

And Mother held my hand and smiled –
I mean the lady would – and she
Would take the woolly blankets off
Her little boy so I could see.

His shut-up eyes would be asleep,
And he would look like our John,
And he would be all crumpled too,
And have a pinkish colour on.

I'd watch his breath go in and out.
His little clothes would all be white.
I'd slip my finger in his hand
To feel how he could hold it tight.

And she would smile and say, 'Take care,'
The mother, Mary, would, 'Take care';
And I would kiss his little hand
And touch his hair.

While Mary put the blankets back
The gentle talk would soon begin.
And when I'd tiptoe softly out
I'd meet the wise men going in.

*Elizabeth Madox Roberts*

## tivity

When God decided to be bones and skin and blood like us
He didn't choose a palace, nothing grand – no frills and fuss.
He slipped in through the back door, with the straw
    and hay and dust.
He just became a baby with no choice but to trust.
And love us without question, as every baby must.

But Creation knew the wonder of this tiny newborn King.
The crystal depths of space were touched, the air itself would sing.
The Word is flesh. The silence of the glittering stars is shattered.
    Heaven rings.
The sky blazed wild with angels, whose song was fire and snow.
When God lay in his mother's arms two thousand years ago.

*Jan Dean*

# Four:
# Who Was There?

### 41. A Child's Christmas Carol

There was a little Baby once
    Born upon Christmas Day;
The oxen lowed His lullabye
    As in His crib He lay:
His tree, it was a lonely tree
    That stood upon a hill,
Its candles were the mighty stars
    That shine upon us still;
His toys were flocks of little lambs,
    He loved to see them play:
It is for Him we are so glad,
    Now upon Christmas Day.

*Christine Chaundler*

## 42. Who Was There?

Who was there that first Christmas day?
Who saw the baby lying in the hay?

'I,' said the cow with the crumpled horn,
'I was there when the baby was born.'

'I,' said the owl, 'from my perch up high,
I heard the baby give his first cry.'

'I,' said the spider, 'as I spun my thread,
I saw Mary stroke the baby's head.'

'I,' said the donkey, 'I was there.
I saw the shepherds kneel in prayer.'

'I,' said the sheep, 'I saw the star
And followed the wise men from afar.'

We all were there that first Christmas day.
We saw the baby asleep in the hay.

*John Foster*

## 43. 'I', Said the Donkey

'I,' said the donkey, all shaggy and brown,
'Carried his mother all into the town,
Carried her uphill, carried her down.
I,' said the donkey, all shaggy and brown.

'I,' said the cow, with spots of red,
'Gave him hay for to rest his head,
Gave a manger for his bed.
I,' said the cow, with spots of red.

'I,' said the sheep, with twisted horn,
'Gave my wool for to keep him warm,
Gave my coat on Christmas morn.
I,' said the sheep with twisted horn.

'I,' said the dove from the rafters high,
'Cooed him to sleep with a lullaby,
Cooed him to sleep my mate and I.
I,' said the dove from the rafters high.

*Anonymous*

## 44. The Barn

'I am tired of this barn,' said the colt.
'And every day it snows.
Outside there's no grass any more
And icicles grow on my nose.
I am tired of hearing the cows
Breathing and talking together.
I am sick of these clucking hens.
I *hate* stables and winter weather!'

'Hush, little colt,' said the mare,
'And a story I will tell
Of a barn like this one of ours
And the wonders that there befell.
It was weather much like this,
And the beasts stood as we stand now
In the warm good dark of the barn –
A horse, and an ass, and a cow.'

'And sheep?' asked the colt. 'Yes, sheep.
And a pig, and a goat, and a hen.
All of the beasts of the barnyard,
The usual servants of men.
And into their midst came a lady
And she was cold as death,
But the animals leaned over her
And made her warm with their breath.

'There was her baby born
And laid to sleep in the hay,
While music flooded the rafters
And the barn was as light as day.
And angels and kings and shepherds
Came to worship the babe from afar,
But we looked at him first of all creatures
By the bright strange light of a star!'

*Elizabeth Coatsworth*

## 45. A Christmas Poem

One of the oxen said
'I know him, he is me – a beast
Of burden, used, abused,
Excluded from the feast –
A toiler, one by whom
No task will be refused:
I wish him strength, I give him room.'

One of the shepherds said
'I know him, he is me – a man
Who wakes when others sleep,
Whose watchful eyes will scan
The drifted snow at night
Alert for the lost sheep:
I give this lamb, I wish him sight.'

One of the wise men said
'I know him, he is me – a king
On wisdom's pilgrimage,
One Plato claimed would bring
The world back to its old
Unclouded golden age:
I wish him truth, I give him gold.'

Mary his mother said
'I know his heart's need, it is mine –
The chosen child who lives
Lost in his Lord's design,
The self and symbol of
The selfless life he gives:
I give him life, I wish him love.'

*Dick Davis*

## 46. In the Stable: Christmas Haiku

*Donkey*
My long ears can hear
Angels singing, but my song
Would wake the baby.

*Dog*
I will not bark but
Lie, head on paws, eyes watching
All these visitors.

*Cat*
I will wash my feet. For
This baby all should be clean.
My purr will soothe him.

*Owl*
My round eyes look down.
No starlit hunting this night:
Peace to little ones!

*Spider*
My fine web sparkles:
Indoor star in the roof's night
Over the baby.

*John Corben*

## 47. Robin

In the stable where the Christ child lay
A small brown bird pecked in the hay
The stable's fire was almost dead
And seeing this, the small bird spread
Its wings out by the last faint spark.
Then, fluttering like a meadowlark,
It fanned it once more into flame.
Good Joseph built the fire again.
Mary, smiling, blessed the bird.
Neither she nor Joseph heard
The bird's faint cries, and neither guessed
At the burnt feathers on its breast.

But when in God's good time new feathers came,
The robin's breast was red as any flame.

*Eric Finney*

## at in the Manger

In the story, I'm not there.
Ox and ass, arranged at prayer:
But me? Nowhere.

Anti-cat evangelists
How on earth could you have missed
Such an obvious and able
Occupant of any stable?

Who excluded mouse and rat?
The harmless necessary cat.
Who snuggled in with the holy pair?
Me. And my purr.

Matthew, Mark, and Luke and John,
(Who got it wrong,
Who left out the cat)
Remember that,
Wherever He went in this great affair
*I* was there.

*U. A. Fanthorpe*

### 49. What the Donkey Saw

No room in the inn, of course,
And not that much in the stable,
What with the shepherds, Magi, Mary,
Joseph, the heavenly host –
Not to mention the baby
Using our manger as a cot.
You couldn't have squeezed another cherub in
For love or money.

Still, in spite of the overcrowding,
I did my best to make them feel wanted.
I could see the baby and I
Would be going places together.

*U. A. Fanthorpe*

## 50. Flight into Egypt

How should I guess
what I was carrying?
So human was the weight
held by his mother
in her cloak and wrappings–
a woman, delicate
after the birth.
How could I tell its value,
or dare to estimate?

I went soft-footed,
for the ground was sodden
with broken mud, sheep droppings,
mist, and snow ...
A strange time to set out
on such a journey –
and where?
To what extremes?
I did not know.

I have thought since:
why, after kings and angels
did they not travel
more like royalty?
But there was no one with us:
just a fellow
twitching the rein,
Mary, the child,
and me.

So we proceed
through a different country,
moving by ways
I had not learned before.
It was hard going ...
neither path nor compass
to lead us ...
only light
from the heart's core.

*Jean Kenward*

# Five:
# Stay Away From The Manger!

## 51. Nativity Play

This year ...
This year can I be Herod?
This year, can I be him?
A wise man
or a Joseph?
An inn man
or a king?

This year ...
can I be famous?
This year, can I be best?
Bear a crown of silver
and wear a golden vest?

This year ...
can I be starlight?
This year, can I stand out? ...
Feel the swish of curtains
and hear the front row shout
'Hurrah' for good old Ronny
he brings a gift of gold
head afire with tinsel

'The Greatest Story Told ...'
'Hurrah for good old Herod!'
and shepherds from afar.

So –
don't make me a palm tree
And can I be –

         a Star?

*Peter Dixon*

## 52. The School Nativity

The shepherds see a blinding light
The cattle come in herds
The little lambs have lost their ears
The angel's lost for words.

The stable starts to shake a bit
A wise man drops his gift
The innkeeper is off with flu
The star begins to drift.

Then Joseph waves to Mum and Dad
Who think their boy's fantastic
Jesus plays it meek and mild, but
Then he would; he's plastic.

*Steve Turner*

## 53. Just Doing My Job

I'm one of Herod's Henchmen.
We don't have much to say,
We just charge through the audience
In a Henchman sort of way.

We all wear woolly helmets
To hide our hair and ears,
And wellingtons sprayed silver
To match our tinfoil spears.

Our swords are made of cardboard
So blood will not be spilled
If we trip and stab a parent
When the hall's completely filled.

We don't look VERY scary,
We're mostly small and shy,
And some of us wear glasses
But we give the thing a try.

We whisper Henchman noises
While Herod hunts for strangers,
And then we all charge out again
Like nervous Power Rangers.

Yet when the play is over
And Miss is out of breath
We'll charge like Henchmen through the hall
And scare our Mums to death.

*Clare Bevan*

## 54. Stay Away from the Manger ( *To the tune of Away in a Manger* )

Stay away from the manger
Is what teacher said
Last year our Lord Jesus
Was dropped on his head
So Mary hit Joseph
Who then tripped a sheep
The shepherds and wise men
Fell down in a heap

The donkey fell over
And rolled off the stage
On to the piano
As Miss turned the page
The lid on her fingers
Came down with a CRACK!
The words that she shouted
Were heard at the back

So this year the infants
Are not in the show
We all said Pleeeaaassse
But teacher said no
Stay away from the manger
You're not going to spoil it
By waving at parents
And wanting the toilet

*Paul Cookson*

# Six:
# The Night Before

## 55. Christmas Eve

Our mother was tearing her hair out,
(My sister and I played upstairs),
There was too much to do,
She would never be through,
And the air was quite blue;
So father had made himself scarce.

He'd been sent to do last-minute shopping
With a list as long as your arm.
Then to us mother said,
'You be useful instead,
Go and clear up the shed –
And leave me some peace to get calm!'

We put on our coats and our wellies
And moaned as we went through the door.
The thick cloud hung low,
And its strange, muddy glow
Held the promise of snow,
And the wind was quite biting and raw.

Our shed wasn't much of a building –
Its door had come off long ago.
What was once a tool-store
Now had cobwebs galore,
Fieldmice under the floor,
And corners where fungus could grow.

We piled things into the middle,
And on top of an old packing case
A basket was laid.
Then we propped up a spade,
Fork, and hoe as we made
A vain effort to tidy the place.

We put dirty rags in the basket,
Dragged over a bag of cement,
From a dusty wire rack
Hauled down bits of sack
And covered the back
Of each garden tool where it leant.

That evening the snow didn't happen,
The sky, full of stars, was aglow.
The moon shone its light
In the shed, and the sight
On that cold Christmas night
Made a wonder much greater than snow.

For it seemed a particular star hung
Just over the shed's wooden gable.
It silvered the floor
And the fine wisps of straw
So our old shed looked more
As if it were really a stable.

What we saw was a group of tall figures
Leaning over the cradle below.
A lamb knelt without sound,
And we looked all around
At the frost on the ground,
Hoping it might be snow.

*Sandy Brownjohn*

## 56. Don't Forget the Birds

A hungry robin
looked for food
in Laura's frosty garden,
bobbed in a fir tree
underneath the eave,

found that the branches
were full of surprises;
'An apple, nuts,
a coconut,
they must be make-believe!'

'Eat up!'
chirped a bluetit
hopped up beside him.
'Laura has remembered us.
Today is Christmas Eve!'

*Irene Rawnsley*

## 57. Christmas Eve

Our
pud is
cooked,
meat stuffed
and rolled –
smells drift of
fruit and almonds
where the cake is
iced and waiting.
Our tree is up, green,
red and gold, and twists
of tinsel shimmer there
from lights illuminating.
Our foil-wrapped secrets to
unfold, and tiptoe stockings hung
with care, are all at once creating,
A feeling that we want to hold suspended
in the tingling air –
It's
called
anticipating.

*Liz Brownlee*

## 58. Christmas Carol

Dress the walls with casuarina
Flaming red poinsettia too,
Mix among them allamanda,
Hibiscus of countless hues
Snow-on-the-mountain, poinciana,
Christmas candles 'cross the door.
Pink and purple bougainvillea,
For it's Christmas-time once more.

Pick the sorrel from the stalk now,
It's that special time of year,
Reap the swollen ginger root and
Make the special ginger beer,
Tangerines are ripe and juicy,
Sweet oranges by the score,
Dig the yams, they'll now be ready,
For it's Christmas-time once more.

*Valerie Bloom*

## 59. You at Christmas

You helped to mix the Christmas cake.
The stirring made your tired arms ache.

You hung the baubles on the tree
till it was glorious to see.

You set the crib out on the shelf
and put the baby in yourself.

You helped to hang the Christmas cards.
It seemed that there were yards and yards.

And, when it came to Christmas eve,
you whispered, 'Yes, I do believe.'

With great excitement in your head
you placed your stocking by your bed.

Then, switching off your bedroom light,
you turned to view the winter night.

And what you saw there caught your eyes
and made you startle with surprise.

No jolly Santa in his sleigh
with reindeer cantering away.

But just a star so silver bright
it seemed to fill the world with light.

And, though so distant in the blue,
it hung and sparkled there for You.

*Tony Mitton*

## 60. Dear Santa ...

I'm writing you this little note
just to say hello.
It's Christmas Eve. I'm in bed, but
I just want you to know
that what I'd like for Christmas is ...
some snow.

Can you do it? Can you try?
Dad says you're really clever.
And I'll leave you a fresh mince pie
and carrots for Rudolf for ever
if, on Christmas Day there's Christmas ...
weather.

I don't want other prezzies,
no board-games, toys or clothes.
But if you've got some sledges,
could you please leave one of those,
so I'm good and ready when ...
it snows.

I want
snow
Santa

Just enough snow for a snowman
and to have a snowball fight,
and by tomorrow morning.
Oh, and the sledge. All right?
Happy Christmas, Santa. Lots of love ...
night, night.

*David Horner*

## 61. Welcome Note

Dear Santa, welcome to our house.
Sorry there's no chimney for you but
a patio door is much less sooty
don't you think?

Please make yourself at home.
Sit down and drink
a modest medium sherry once again.
Try not to let it dribble down your chin;
it marked the table last year (note the stain).

I baked the mince pies fresh today.
Have one or two, but there again take care –
I want No Crumbs, because, you see, last year,
regretfully, I found them everywhere.

You'll find the children's stockings by their beds.
Be more sensible than usual – nothing loud.
No monkey this time please, or anything
that makes a mess.

I hope you've read the notice on the door
and left your boots out on the patio. Last year –
Muddy Footprints Everywhere.
All Christmas Day I scrubbed the carpet but
if you look closely you'll see they're still there.

Last, and I most sincerely hope you'll pardon
any offence this causes them, but reindeer
aren't the most fastidious of eaters are they?
I must insist they crunch their carrots
IN THE GARDEN.

So make yourself at home, be of good cheer.
Thanks for coming.
Have a lovely year.

*Frances Nagle*

## 62. If

If I were Father Christmas
I'd deliver all my toys
By rocket ship, a sleigh's too slow
For eager girls and boys,
I'd nip down every chimney-pot
And never miss a roof,
While Rudolph worked the ship's controls
With antler tip and hoof.

*Richard Edwards*

## 63. Questions on Christmas Eve

But *how* can his reindeer fly without wings?
Jets on their hooves? That's plain cheating!
And *how* can he climb down the chimney pot
    When we've got central heating?

You say it's all magic and I shouldn't ask
About Santa on Christmas Eve.
But I'm confused by the stories I've heard;
    I don't know what to believe.

I said that I'd sit up in bed all night long
To see if he really would call.
But I fell fast asleep, woke up after dawn
　　As something banged in the hall.

I saw my sock crammed with apples and sweets;
There were parcels piled high near the door.
Jingle bells tinkled far off in the dark:
　　One snowflake shone on the floor.

*Wes Magee*


## 64. You Do Not Need a Chimney for Santa Claus to Come

You do not need a chimney
for Santa Claus to come
You do not need a fireplace
to hang your stocking from

That stuff is just from tele
Do not believe the films
You do not need a great big house
for Santa to come in

He's got a sleigh, for goodness sake
and loads of elves at hand;
Mrs Claus behind the scenes
computing all the plans;
Flying, glowing reindeer
galloping the Christmas air

Of course he can manage
a few quick flights of stairs –

the top flat of a tower block;
a barge on a canal;
the spare room of a friend's house;
a hostel; a hotel

So snuggle into sleep now
and don't listen to anyone
who says you need a chimney
for Santa Claus to come

*Hollie McNish*

## 65. A Visit from St Nicholas

'Twas the night before Christmas, when all through the house
Not a creature was stirring, not even a mouse;
The stockings were hung by the chimney with care,
In hopes that St Nicholas soon would be there;
The children were nestled all snug in their beds,
While visions of sugarplums danced in their heads;

And Mamma in her 'kerchief, and I in my cap,
Had just settled our brains for a long winter's nap;
When out on the lawn there arose such a clatter,
I sprang from the bed to see what was the matter.
Away to the window I flew like a flash,
Tore open the shutters and threw up the sash.

The moon, on the breast of the new-fallen snow,
Gave the lustre of midday to objects below,
When what to my wondering eyes should appear,
But a miniature sleigh, and eight tiny reindeer,
With a little old driver, so lively and quick,
I knew in a moment it must be St Nick.

More rapid than eagles his coursers they came,
And he whistled and shouted, and called them by name:
'Now, Dasher! Now, Dancer! Now, Prancer and Vixen!
On, Comet! On, Cupid! On, Donner and Blitzen!
To the top of the porch! To the top of the wall!
Now, dash away! Dash away! Dash away all!'

As dry leaves that before the wild hurricane fly,
When they meet with an obstacle, mount to the sky;
So up to the housetop the coursers they flew,
With the sleigh full of toys, and St Nicholas too.
And then, in a twinkling, I heard on the roof
The prancing and pawing of each little hoof –
As I drew in my head, and was turning around,
Down the chimney St Nicholas came with a bound.

He was dressed all in fur, from his head to his foot,
And his clothes were all tarnished with ashes and soot;
A bundle of toys he had flung on his back,
And he looked like a pedlar just opening his pack.
His eyes – how they twinkled! His dimples, how merry!
His cheeks were like roses, his nose like a cherry!

His droll little mouth was drawn up like a bow,
And the beard on his chin was as white as the snow;
The stump of a pipe he held tight in his teeth,
And the smoke it encircled his head like a wreath;
He had a broad face and a little round belly
That shook, when he laughed, like a bowl full of jelly.

He was chubby and plump, a right jolly old elf,
And I laughed, when I saw him, in spite of myself;
A wink of his eye and a twist of his head
Soon gave me to know I had nothing to dread;
He spoke not a word, but went straight to his work,
And filled all the stockings; then turned with a jerk,

And laying his finger aside of his nose,
And giving a nod, up the chimney he rose;
He sprang to his sleigh, to his team gave a whistle,
And away they all flew like the down of a thistle.
But I heard him exclaim, ere he drove out of sight,
*'Happy Christmas to all, and to all a good night!'*

*Clement Clarke Moore*

## 66. Christmas Limerick

There once was a greedy young elf
who kept Santa's gifts for himself.
He made quite a name
for in time he became
an elf of exceptional welf.

*Trevor Parsons*

## 67.  Alternative Santa

'I'm fed up looking like Father Christmas,'
Muttered Father Christmas one year.
'I need a new outfit. I must move with the times.
So, for a start, it's goodbye, reindeer.'
He googled 'alternative Santas'
And was amazed at the stuff that appeared.
He got rid of the holly-red costume,
Had a haircut, and shaved off his beard.
Spent weeks in front of a computer
In a cave hollowed out of the ice
Wearing a T-shirt emblazoned HAPPY HOLIDAY
And jeans (Amazon, half price).
Couldn't wait to straddle his snow-ped
(The bargain he'd bought on eBay):
A rocket-powered silver toboggan,
His supersonic sleigh.
Then one morning he thought, 'Oh why bother
Delivering presents by hand
When it could all be done online?
Busy parents will understand.
We are lucky to live in a digital age
Where the aim is access and speed.
SantaNet I'll call the system –
Santafaction guaranteed.'

And that was years and years ago
Now little children barely know
About midnight mass and mistletoe
Christmas carols and candle glow
Sleigh bells ringing across the snow
And Santa singing Yo Ho Ho
For that was years and years ago
For that was years and years ago.

*Roger McGough*

# Seven:
# Celebrate The Day

### 68. In Far-off Lands and Near

In a snow-wrapped land of the north,
far, far away,
icicle lanterns glow from firs
to celebrate the Day.

In a sun-trapped land of the south,
far, far away,
children sing on golden sands
to celebrate the Day.

In a cloud-lapped land between,
not so far away,
candles burn and carols ring
as *we* celebrate the Day.

*Judith Nicholls*

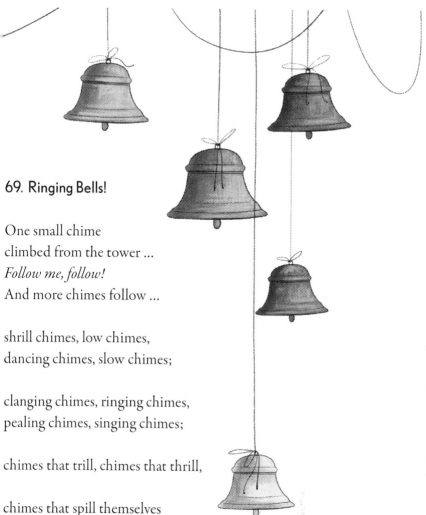

## 69. Ringing Bells!

One small chime
climbed from the tower ...
*Follow me, follow!*
And more chimes follow ...

shrill chimes, low chimes,
dancing chimes, slow chimes;

clanging chimes, ringing chimes,
pealing chimes, singing chimes;

chimes that trill, chimes that thrill,

chimes that spill themselves
over forests and rooftops
filling the earth and the skies,
filling the sky and the earth
with their Christmas message:

*This is the Day of Jesus' birth!*

*Judith Nicholls*

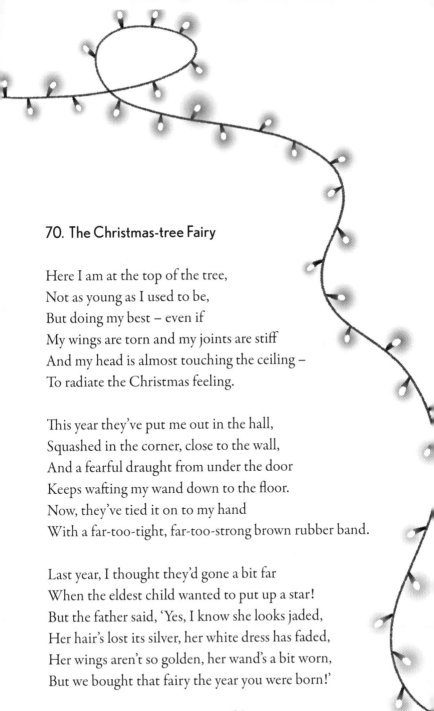

## 70. The Christmas-tree Fairy

Here I am at the top of the tree,
Not as young as I used to be,
But doing my best – even if
My wings are torn and my joints are stiff
And my head is almost touching the ceiling –
To radiate the Christmas feeling.

This year they've put me out in the hall,
Squashed in the corner, close to the wall,
And a fearful draught from under the door
Keeps wafting my wand down to the floor.
Now, they've tied it on to my hand
With a far-too-tight, far-too-strong brown rubber band.

Last year, I thought they'd gone a bit far
When the eldest child wanted to put up a star!
But the father said, 'Yes, I know she looks jaded,
Her hair's lost its silver, her white dress has faded,
Her wings aren't so golden, her wand's a bit worn,
But we bought that fairy the year you were born!'

So here I am at the top of the tree,
Not the most comfortable place to be –
No one knows how the pine needles prickle,
No one would guess how the tinsel can tickle –
But while I'm up here, I know my place
And nothing can alter the smile on my face!

*June Crebbin*


## 71. Drawback

The fairy on top of the Christmas tree
Said, 'I hate my job, it's rotten –
How would you like it, perched up here
With pine needles stuck up your bottom?'

*Clive Webster*

## 72. Baffled Turkey

Last night they brought a tree home,
They took it into the hall,
Now why would they do a thing like that?
I don't understand it at all.

Now they're hanging some tinsel upon it,
Some coloured streamers and balls,
And long loopy ribbons of twinkling lights,
I don't understand it at all.

There's a red and green circle on the front door,
And mistletoe on the wall,
And the farmer's inspecting a red and white suit,
I don't understand it at all.

Out on the porch they're erecting
What looks like a manger and stall,
With a stuffed donkey, a baby, and three kings,
I don't understand it at all.

Lately they've given me so much to eat,
I'm almost as round as a ball,
And now they are taking me up to the house,
I don't understand it, at all.

*Valerie Bloom*

## 73. Talking Turkeys!!

Be nice to yu turkeys dis christmas
Cos turkeys jus wanna hav fun
Turkeys are cool, turkeys are wicked
An every turkey has a Mum.
Be nice to yu turkeys dis christmas,
Don't eat it, keep it alive,
It could be yu mate an not on yu plate
Say, Yo! Turkey I'm on your side.

I got lots of friends who are turkeys
An all of dem fear christmas time,
Dey wanna enjoy it, dey say humans destroyed it
An humans are out of dere mind,
Yeah, I got lots of friends who are turkeys
Dey all hav a right to a life,
Not to be caged up an genetically made up
By any farmer an his wife.

Turkeys jus wanna play reggae
Turkeys jus wanna hip-hop
Can yu imagine a nice young turkey saying,
'I cannot wait for de chop'?
Turkeys like getting presents, dey wanna watch christmas TV,
Turkeys hav brains an turkeys feel pain
In many ways like yu an me.

I once knew a turkey called
Turkey
He said, 'Benji explain to me please,
Who put de turkey in christmas
An what happens to christmas trees?'
I said, 'I am not too sure turkey
But it's nothing to do wid Christ Mass
Humans get greedy an waste more dan need be
An business men mek loadsa cash.'

Be nice to yu turkey dis christmas
Invite dem indoors fe sum greens
Let dem eat cake an let dem partake
In a plate of organic grown beans,
Be nice to yu turkey dis christmas
An spare dem de cut of de knife,
Join Turkeys United an dey'll be delighted
An yu will mek new friends **'FOR LIFE'**.

*Benjamin Zephaniah*

## 74. Reggie

A very fat turkey named Reggie
At Christmas became rather edgy,
He was huffin' and puffin'
At the mere thought of stuffin'
– How he wished everyone was a 'veggie'.

*Colin West*


## 75. Santa Claws

I don't know why they're blaming me
When all I did was climb a tree
And bat a shiny silver ball.
How could I know the tree would fall?
And when those silly lights went out
They didn't have to scream and shout
And turf me out and shut the door.
Now no one loves me any more.
I'm in the kitchen by myself.
But wait! What's on that high-up shelf?
A lovely turkey, big and fat!
How nice! They *do* still love their cat.

*Julia Donaldson*

## 76.  Turkey Surprise

Now Christmas lunch is quite a treat
With crackers, hats and lots to eat
But every year mum buys a bird
The size of which is quite absurd.

Fifteen pounds of turkey meat
Is far too much for three to eat
Yet every year she does the same
She plays her outsized turkey game.

Now as I've said it's quite a treat
This splendid lunch with lots to eat,
But that which follows makes us cringe
It's mother's five day turkey binge.

There's turkey rissoles, turkey stew,
Turkey broth and curry too
Turkey burgers, cold turkey thighs
Not to mention turkey surprise.

Now come on mum, enough's enough!
We've had our fill of turkey stuff
Please listen to us, mother dear,
And buy an eight pound bird next year.

*Richard Caley*

## 77. Edible Angels

You can talk of hot roast turkey
   with skin that's golden brown.
You can pray for Christmas pudding
   with cream that dribbles down.

You can murmur on for warm mince pies
   that crumble as you bite.
But for me there is one special thing
   I think of with delight.

You can dream of hot potatoes
   and steaming sprouts, of course.
You can sing of dark, rich gravy
   and scrumptious, thick bread sauce.

But, when it comes to Christmas,
   the things that sing to me
are the little chocolate angels
   that swing upon the tree.

*Tony Mitton*

## 78. Christmas Crackers

I rattle the cracker to my ear
When it's pulled what will appear –
A riddle, a whistle, a paper hat?
The contents will bore me, that's a fact

Last year my hat split on my head
And my riddle was stupid it must be said
– What goes up when the rain comes down? –
And a plastic ring the worst in town

But still every year the crackers are placed
We all know this moment must be faced
But though I pretend it's really fun
I'm hungry for my dinner so let's get it done

*Janet Greenyer*

## 79.  The Father Christmas on the Cake

For fifty weeks I've languished
Upon the cupboard shelf,
Forgotten and uncared for,
I've muttered to myself.
But now the year is closing
And Christmastime is here,
They dust me down and tell me
To show a little cheer.
Between the plaster snowman
And little glassy lake
They stand me in the middle
Of some ice-covered cake,
And for a while there's laughter,
But as the week wears on,
They cut up all the landscape
Till every scrap is gone.
Then with the plaster snowman
And little lake of glass
I'm banished to the cupboard
For one more year to pass.

*Colin West*

## 80. Auntie Mimi's Mistletoe

Auntie Mimi's mistletoe,
She ties it to her head
And goes round kissing everyone,
She's kissed my uncle Fred,
She's kissed my mum, she's kissed my dad,
The postman, and the cat,
She kissed the man next door so hard
She squashed his glasses flat,
She's kissed my little brother,
Though he hid behind the tree,
And now she's coming my way
But she won't get me!

*Richard Edwards*

## 81. Blue Christmas

I'm having a lousy Christmas
Not even a robin in sight,
There's a great big hole in my stocking,
And I've just fused the Christmas tree lights.

The dog is away in the manger,
Even the pudding won't light;
Singing Merry Christmas
On this all-too-silent night.

Good King Wenceslas looked out
Over a year ago:
How can I follow his footsteps
When there isn't any snow?

The mistletoe's getting all dusty
With no one there to kiss,
Even the mince pies taste musty:
Can New Year be worse than this?

*Adrian Henri*

## 82. Christmas Invitation

Sally had an elephant
Soft and pink and blue,
Auntie had a petticoat
And Arthur had the 'flu.

Janice had a pretty hat
Friskie had a bone,
Granny had a headache
And Uncle had a moan.

Billy had a bellyache
The salmon tasted tinned,
Bertie had an argument
And Walter had the wind.

Minnie had a nasty turn
Mother had a weep,
Uncle had the whisky
And Auntie fell asleep.

Colin had a hacking cough
Cathy had a fit
Uncle had a tummy ache
And the baby had a nit.

Mildred had a lie-down
The telly got the blink,
Auntie made a trifle
And Uncle made a stink.

Mavis had a big 'to do'
– Someone squashed her hat,
Auntie saw the future
And Uncle saw a rat.

Frankie had a funny knee
Daisy had a corn,
Bob had awful rumbles
And Harry had the yawns.

Oh, we had a lovely Christmas
Relations are such FUN ...

So here's an

Invitation

Next year ...
Yes ...

You can come!

*Clive Webster*

# Eight:
# The Price Of Presents

## 83. Barely Worth It

Relatives descend.
Wet kisses and questions are
the price of presents.

*Ted Scheu*

## 84. Dave Dirt's Christmas Presents

Dave Dirt wrapped his Christmas presents
Late on Christmas Eve
And gave his near relations things
That you would not believe.

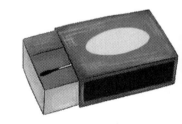

His brother got an Odour-Eater –
Second-hand one, natch.
For Dad he chose, inside its box,
A single burnt-out match.

His sister copped the sweepings from
His hairy bedroom rug,
While Mum received a centipede
And Granny got a slug.

Next day he had the nerve to sit
Beneath the Christmas tree
And say: 'OK, I've done my bit –
What have you got for me?'

*Kit Wright*

## 85. What Not to Buy Me

Don't buy me knickers
Don't buy me socks
Don't give me small things
Inside a big box.

Don't buy me brushes
Don't buy a comb
Don't buy me schoolbooks
To work on at home

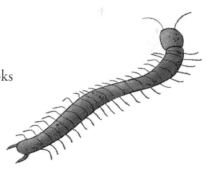

Don't buy me ribbons
Don't buy me bows
Don't buy me tissues
To dab at my nose

Don't buy me stickers
Don't buy me stamps
Don't buy me paper
For letters of thanks

Don't buy me dusters
Don't buy me spray
Don't buy me cleaners
That take stains away

Don't buy me cufflinks
Don't buy me ties
Don't buy me earmuffs.
Buy me: a surprise.

*Steve Turner*

## 86. Christmas Thank Yous

Dear Auntie
Oh, what a nice jumper
I've always adored powder blue
and fancy you thinking of
orange and pink
for the stripes
how clever of you!

Dear Uncle
The soap is
terrific
So
useful
and such a kind thought and
how did you guess that
I'd just used the last of
the soap that last Christmas brought

Dear Gran
Many thanks for the hankies
Now I really can't wait for the flu
and the daisies embroidered
in red round the 'M'
for Michael
how
thoughtful of you!

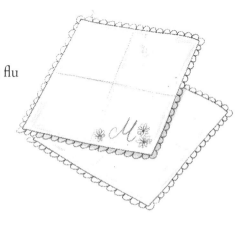

Dear Cousin
What socks!
and the same sort you wear
so you must be
the last word in style
and I'm certain you're right that the
luminous green
*will* make me stand out a mile

Dear Sister
I quite understand your concern
it's a risk sending jam in the post
But I think I've pulled out
all the big bits
of glass
so it won't taste too sharp
spread on toast

Dear Grandad
Don't fret
I'm delighted
So *don't* think your gift will
offend
I'm not at all hurt
that you gave up this year
and just sent me
a fiver
to spend

*Mick Gowar*

## 87. On the Thirteenth Day of Christmas My True Love Phoned Me Up ...

Well, I suppose I should be grateful, you've obviously gone
to a lot of trouble and expense – or maybe off your head.
Yes, I did like the birds – the small ones anyway were fun
if rather messy, but now the hens have roosted on my bed
and the rest are nested on the wardrobe. It's hard to sleep
with all that cooing, let alone the cackling of the geese
whose eggs are everywhere, but mostly in a broken smelly heap
on the sofa. No, why should I mind? I can't get any peace
anywhere – the lounge is full of drummers thumping tom-toms
and sprawling lords crashed out from manic leaping. The kitchen
is crammed with cows and milkmaids and smells of a million
    stink-bombs
and enough sour milk to last a year. The pipers? I'd forgotten them –
they were no trouble, I paid them and they went. But I can't get rid
of these young ladies. They won't stop dancing or turn
    the music down
and they're always in the bathroom, squealing as they skid
across the flooded floor. No, I don't need a plumber round,
it's just the swans – where else can they swim? Poor things,
I think they're going mad, like me. When I went to wash my
hands one ate the soap, another swallowed the gold rings.
And the pear tree died. Too dry. So thanks for nothing, love.
Goodbye.

*Dave Calder*

115

## 88. My Mum Is Nicer Than I Am

when i ask my mum
what she wants from me for Christmas
every year she says the same:

'i've got everything I want
just a hug will do me fine'

and every year she smiles, and says:
'and what can I get you?'

and I feel bad
cos hugs are nice and that
but I'm wanting presents too

*Hollie McNish*

# Nine:
# What Christmas Is For

## 89. It Started with a Baby

It started with a Baby
and a manger, soft with hay.
It started with three Kings
who came from far away.
It started with some shepherds
who saw angels, tall and bright.
It started with a brilliant star
which filled the skies with light.
Now Christmas trees are sparkling
and the shops are filled with toys
which will shortly be delivered
to happy girls and boys.

Toddlers wait for Father Christmas
with his reindeer and his sleigh,
Christmas cards are posted
and, on Christmas Day,
there's the opening of the presents
and the Christmas games and fun,
but, later on, at bedtime
when Christmas Day is done
remember how it started,
with a Baby, in the hay,
in a manger, in a stable,
two thousand years away.

*Marian Swinger*

## 90. Cradle Song

Sweet dreams form a shade
O'er my lovely infant's head:
Sweet dreams of pleasant streams
By happy, silent moony beams.

Sweet sleep with soft down
Weave thy brows an infant crown;
Sweet sleep, angel mild,
Hover o'er my happy child.

Sweet smiles in the night,
Hover over my delight;
Sweet smiles, mother's smiles,
All the livelong night beguiles.

Sweet moans, dovelike sighs,
Chase not slumber from thy eyes;
Sweet moans, sweeter smiles;
All the dovelike moans beguiles.

Sleep, sleep, happy child;
All creation slept and smiled;
Sleep, sleep, happy sleep,
While o'er thee thy mother weep.

Sweet babe, in thy face
Holy image I can trace:
Sweet babe, once like thee
Thy Maker lay and wept for me.

Wept for me, for thee, for all
When He was an infant small:
Thou His image ever see,
Heavenly face that smiles on thee.

Smiles on me, on thee, on all,
Who became an infant small:
Infant smiles are His own smiles
Heaven and earth to peace beguiles.

*William Blake*

120

## 91. Christmas Landscape

Tonight the wind gnaws
with teeth of glass,
the jackdaw shivers
in caged branches of iron,
the stars have talons.

There is hunger in the mouth
of vole and badger,
silver agonies of breath
in the nostril of the fox,
ice on the rabbit's paw.

Tonight has no moon,
no food for the pilgrim;
the fruit tree is bare,
the rose bush a thorn
and the ground is bitter with stones.

But the mole sleeps, and the hedgehog
lies curled in a womb of leaves,
the bean and the wheat-seed
hug their germs in the earth
and the stream moves under the ice.

Tonight there is no moon,
but a new star opens
like a silver trumpet over the dead.
Tonight in a nest of ruins
the blessèd babe is laid.

And the fir tree warms to a bloom of candles,
the child lights his lantern,
stares at his tinselled toy;
our hearts and hearths
smoulder with live ashes.

In the blood of our grief
the cold earth is suckled,
in our agony the womb
convulses its seed,
in the cry of anguish
the child's first breath is born.

*Laurie Lee*

## 92. The Child and the Beggar

A white carpet for Winter
And a crackling of frost,
A Christmas card picture
Whose beauty is lost
On the man in the doorway
Who shivers and prays
For a change in the weather,
The sun's pallid rays.

Wind cuts every corner
To savage the poor
Through cracks in the shutters
And under the door:
The new-born child shivers
And cries with the cold;
Even if he survives
He will never grow old.

The child and the beggar
Live under one star
That illumines creation
Wherever we are:
Give warmth to the beggar
In the infant child's name:
Praise God in your kindness
In thanks that he came.

*Kevin Carey*

## 93. What Do You Want for Christmas?

'For Christmas, would you like some gold?'
*I'd rather just have money.*
'And what about some frankincense?'
*Come on, you're being funny.*

*And what is more, I don't want ...* 'No!
I've gone and bought the myrrh!'
*You could have asked me for a list*
*of things that I'd prefer.*

'You're not exactly Jesus then?'
*Oh, no. I'm plain old me.*
*And I want fairly normal gifts*
*left underneath the tree:*

*I'll have this season's latest fad,*
*to be like all my friends*
*And chocolate that will last me, oh,*
*at least till this year ends.*

'But Christmas gifts should be much more –
they should have lasting worth.'
*May I suggest good will to all*
*and maybe peace on earth.*

*Lois Rock*

124

## 94. What Did You Get for Christmas?

This is far fantastical,
the best night-ever-magical,
the heart of this strange madrigal
... a baby born in straw.
This winter anniversary,
this cracker of festivity,
a most unlikely birthday spree,
this fortune for the poor.
This hoopla, shindig, jubilee,
with cartwheels through-the-streets-whoopee,
this liberty nativity,
the start of so much more.
This wingding gift of revelry ...
... the stable as a Christmas tree,
red carpet inclusivity
for all, for you, for me ...
... The night sky's vast fluorescence,
Royal, cosmic effervescence,
our present of the Presence ...
... for all, for you, for me.

*Stewart Henderson*

## 95. The Sky Is Black Tonight

The sky is black tonight;
Coal-black, crow-black,
But in that black
Is the white-bright light
Of a star.

That star has a gift tonight:
A birth-gift, a for-all-the-earth gift.
For in that star
Is a fly-by-night:
Is a bird.

That bird has a song tonight:
A love-song, high-above song.
And in that song
Is the silver tongue
Of a bell.

That bell has a wish tonight;
A bell-wish, a well-wish.
And the wish
In the bell
In the song
In the bird
In the star
In the black
In the sky
Is Peace,
Is Peace,
Is Peace.

*Berlie Doherty*

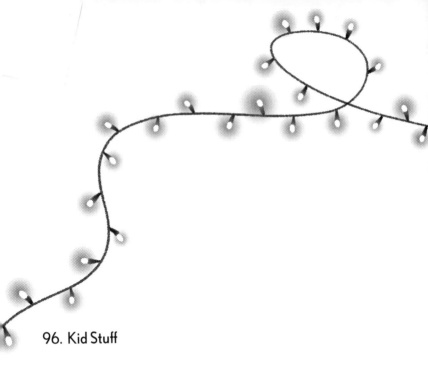

## 96. Kid Stuff

The wise guys
Tell me
That Christmas
Is Kid Stuff ...
Maybe they've got
something there –
Two thousand years ago
three wise guys
chase a star
across a continent
to bring
frankincense and myrrh
to a Kid
born in a manger
with an idea in his head ...

And as the bombs
crash
all over the world today
the real wise guys know
that we've all got to go
chasing stars
again
in the hope
that we can get back
some of that
Kid Stuff
Born two thousand years ago.

*Frank Horne*

## 97. A Martian Christmas

After a long year and a half in space,
We reached Mars –
December 25th, 2033!
Christmas dinner was all planned –
Freeze-dried turkey and roast potatoes,
With Christmas pud squeezed from a tube to follow.
Presents were a problem –
We hadn't been able to stop off
For shopping on the way.

And we went outside for the first time,
And got depressed.
Sand, nothing but sand.
'Maybe the three wise men
Will come plodding round that sand dune
On their camels,'
Someone said, but we didn't laugh.
We were too busy thinking about Christmas,
But that was fifty million miles away.

Then we saw the star,
Hanging like a lantern in the east.
'It's Earth,' someone said.
We just looked and looked –
It must have been the brightness of it
That made our eyes water.

*David Orme*

## 98. Three Christmas Wishes

If I had three Christmas wishes
My first wish would be
For an end to hunger and poverty.

If I had three Christmas wishes
My second would be for
An end to violence, hatred, and war.

If I had three Christmas wishes
My third wish would be
That we take proper care of the land and the sea.

*John Foster*


## 99. Christmas for Free

Christmas is expensive, my grandma said to me,
Except for Christmas starlight – that shines on earth for free,
And frost like silver tinsel on every woodland tree
And all the love that we can share together, you and me.

*Lois Rock*

## 100. What Christmas Is For

Christmas is a time for gifts –
For giving and for getting.

Christmas is a time for peace –
Forgiving and forgetting.

*Philip Waddell*

# INDEX OF POEMS

# INDEX OF POETS

# ACKNOWLEDGEMENTS

SPCK is grateful to all who have granted permission to reproduce poems still in copyright, as follows.

**1** Curtis Brown for 'Winter Morning' © Ogden Nash.
**3** 'The Coming of the Cold', 1941 by Theodore Roethke; from *Collected Poems* by Theodore Roethke. Used by permission of Doubleday, an imprint of the Knopf Doubleday Publishing Group, a division of Penguin Random House LLC. All rights reserved. Reproduced by permission of Faber and Faber Ltd.
**6** 'The Christmas Life' by Wendy Cope. Reproduced by permission of Faber and Faber Ltd.
**7 & 38** Reproduced by permission of the author, Coral Rumble.
**10**, **20 & 63** Reproduced by permission of the author, Wes Magee.
**11** 'At Nine of the Night' by Charles Causley from *Bring in the Holly* (Frances Lincoln Children's Books), reproduced by permission of David Higham Associates Limited.
**12** 'Snow and Snow' by Ted Hughes. Reproduced by permission of Faber and Faber Ltd.
**13** 'First Snow in the Street' by Brian Patten. Copyright © Brian Patten. Reproduced by permission of the author c/o Rogers, Coleridge & White Ltd, 20 Powis Mews, London W11 1JN.
**14 & 19** 'Winter Morning' and 'The Land of Snow' by Clive Sansom, reproduced by permission of David Higham Associates Limited.
**21, 22, 27 & 53** Reproduced by permission of the author, Clare Bevan.
**23 & 67** Reproduced by permission of the author, Roger McGough.
**24** 'Mary's Burden' by Eleanor Farjeon from *Silver Sand and Snow* (Michael Joseph), reproduced by permission of David Higham Associates Limited.
**26** 'Something Beautiful and New and Strange' by Clive Sansom from *The Witnesses and Other Poems* (Methuen), reproduced by permission of David Higham Associates Limited.

Printed in the United States
by Baker & Taylor Publisher Services